RETRIEVERS

Valerie Bodden

Creative Education

published by Creative Education
P.O. Box 227, Mankato, Minnesota 56002
Creative Education is an imprint of
The Creative Company
www.thecreativecompany.us

design and production by
Christine Vanderbeek
art direction by Rita Marshall
printed in the United States of America

photographs by Alamy (AF archive,
Moviestore collection Ltd, Photos 12),
iStockphoto (Nathan Allred, Leslie
Banks, Eriklam, Jon Huelskamp, rusm),
Shutterstock (Russ Beinder, Margarita
Borodina, Volodymyr Burdiak, Eric Isselee,
JPagetRFPhotos, Dmitry Kalinovsky, Robert
Kneschke, Neveshkin Nikolay, Viorel Sima,
Nikolai Tsvetkov, USBFCO, WilleeCole),
Christine Vanderbeek

library of congress
cataloging-in-publication data
Bodden, Valerie.
Retrievers / Valerie Bodden.
p. cm. — (Fetch!)
SUMMARY: A brief overview of the physical
characteristics, personality traits, and habits
of the retriever breeds, as well as descriptions
of famous pop-culture retrievers such
as Buddy.
Includes index.

ISBN 978-1-60818-364-7
1. Retrievers—Juvenile literature. I. Title.
SF429.R4B58 2014
636.752'7—dc23   2013005520

first edition
9 8 7 6 5 4 3 2 1

TABLE OF CONTENTS

RUNNING RETRIEVERS

Retrievers are **breeds** of dogs. Retrievers are friendly and smart. They like to run! Retrievers love to please their owners, too.

WHAT DO RETRIEVERS LOOK LIKE?

There are many different breeds of retrievers. Labrador retrievers are some of the most popular. They have a wide head and long ears. Golden retrievers are popular, too. They have long tails.

Golden (above) and Labrador (right) are two favorite retriever breeds.

Most retrievers weigh between 55 and 80 pounds (25–36 kg). They are 18 to 27 inches (46–69 cm) tall. Labrador retrievers have short fur. The fur can be yellow, black, or chocolate (brown). Golden retrievers have long, golden fur on their neck, belly, and tail. Retrievers have **water-resistant** fur.

Retrievers can get wet without being soaked all the way through.

RETRIEVER PUPPIES

Newborn retrievers usually weigh about one pound (0.5 kg). But they grow fast! The fur of some retrievers changes color as the dog gets older. Golden retrievers get darker as the puppy grows up.

Retriever puppies can be clumsy but are full of energy.

RETRIEVERS IN MOVIES

Retrievers can be seen in many movies. The movie *Old Yeller* stars a dog that is part yellow lab and part *mastiff*. The movie *Homeward Bound* tells the story of a golden retriever named Shadow who travels across the country with a cat and an American bulldog.

Old Yeller (below) and Shadow the golden retriever (right).

Fetch!

RETRIEVERS AND PEOPLE

People have used retrievers to hunt for more than 100 years. A retriever's job is to retrieve, or bring back, a bird that has been shot. Other retrievers help guide **blind** people or work as **therapy dogs**. Some retrievers serve as search-and-rescue dogs, too.

Retrievers work well with people because they love to please.

Fetch!

Most retrievers are very good with kids. Retriever puppies can make good pets. But puppies can be too active for some people. Adult retrievers are calmer. But they might have some bad habits. Both male and female retrievers make good pets. Females are usually smaller than males.

Retrievers need to be trained as puppies so that they don't learn bad habits (left).

Fetch!

WHAT DO RETRIEVERS LIKE TO DO?

Most retrievers like to live indoors with their family.

But they need lots of exercise outdoors every day.

Retrievers need to be brushed at least once a week.

Retrievers need to be able to run around and play outside (right).

Fetch!

Retrievers love to play with their owners. Throw a ball for your retriever. She will bring it back to you again and again. You will both have fun!

A FAMOUS RETRIEVER

Buddy was a stray golden retriever who became the star of the 1997 movie *Air Bud*. In the movie, Buddy escapes from his mean owner and is found by a 12-year-old boy named Josh. The boy discovers that Buddy can play basketball. At the end of the movie, Buddy helps Josh's team win the championship basketball game.

GLOSSARY

blind unable to see

breeds kinds of an animal with certain traits, such as long ears or a good nose

mastiff a big breed of dog, with a short coat and hanging lips

therapy dogs dogs that help people who are sick or hurt by letting the people pet and enjoy them

water-resistant able to keep water off

READ MORE

Johnson, Jinny. *Golden Retriever*. North Mankato, Minn.: Smart Apple Media, 2004.

Schuh, Mari C. *Golden Retrievers*. Minneapolis: Bellwether Media, 2009.

———. *Labrador Retrievers*. Minneapolis: Bellwether Media, 2009.

WEBSITES

Bailey's Responsible Dog Owner's Coloring Book
http://classic.akc.org/pdfs/public_education/coloring_book.pdf
Print out pictures to color, and learn more about caring for a pet dog.

Just Dog Breeds: Labrador Retriever
http://www.justdogbreeds.com/labrador-retriever.html
Learn more about Labrador retrievers, and check out lots of retriever pictures.

Every effort has been made to ensure that these sites are suitable for children, that they have educational value, and that they contain no inappropriate material. However, because of the nature of the Internet, it is impossible to guarantee that these sites will remain active indefinitely or that their contents will not be altered.

INDEX